✔ KU-274-923

HORRIBLE HISTORIES.

TERRY DEARY

ILLUSTRATED BY
MARTIN BROWN

UP IN THE AIR

READ ALL ABOUT THE NASTY BITS!

EEK!

SCHOLASTIC

While this book is based on real characters and actual historical events, some situations and people are fictional. The 'advertisements' * are entirely fictional and do not relate to any actual service or product and are not intended imply they or anything similar may exist. No 'advertisement' constitutes an endorsement, guarantee, warranty or recommendation by the publisher and the publisher does not make representations or warranties about any product or service contained or implied to be contained therein.

* except any advertisements for the publisher's books that is

Published in the UK by Scholastic Children's Books, 2021
Euston House, 24 Eversholt Street, London, NW1 1DB
Scholastic Ltd Ireland offices at: Unit 89E, Lagan Road,
Dublin Industrial Estate, Glasnevin, Dublin 11.
A division of Scholastic Limited

London ~ New York ~ Toronto ~ Sydney ~ Auckland
Mexico City ~ New Delhi ~ Hong Kong

SCHOLASTIC and associated logos are trademarks and/or registered trademarks of Scholastic Inc.

Text © Terry Deary, 2021
Illustrations © Martin Brown, 2021

The right of Terry Deary and Martin Brown to be identified as the author and illustrators of this work respectively has been asserted by them in accordance with the Copyright, Designs and Patents Act, 1988.

ISBN 978 0702 30585 6

A CIP catalogue record for this book is available from the British Library.

All rights reserved.
This book is sold subject to the condition that it shall not, by way of trade or otherwise, be lent, hired out or otherwise circulated in any form of binding or cover other than that in which it is published. No part of this publication may be reproduced, stored in a retrieval system, or transmitted in any form or by any other means (electronic, mechanical, photocopying, recording or otherwise) without prior written permission of Scholastic Limited.

Printed and bound in the UK by CPI Group (UK) Ltd, Croydon, CR0 4YY
Papers used by Scholastic Children's Books are made from wood grown in sustainable forests.

2 4 6 8 10 9 7 5 3 1

www.scholastic.co.uk

WHAT'S INSIDE?

The WORLD'S FIRST AEROPLANE See page 29

MAKE YOUR OWN PARACHUTE See page 54

INTRODUCTION see page 7

KITES see page 10

JUMPERS see page 15

BALLOONS see page 22

GLIDERS see page 37

PARACHUTES see page 44

PRIZES see page 56

POWERED FLIGHT see page 74

The First World War see page 84

THE GOLDEN AGE see page 97

SECOND WORLD WAR see page 122

EPILOGUE see page 134

INTERESTING INDEX see page 139

INTRODUCTION

What is the safest way to travel?

By air, of course.

Each year, one person in 11 million dies in an air accident.

It is five times more dangerous to fall out of bed. Every year in Britain 20 people die after falling out of bed. Scaredy-cats can sleep on the floor.

ROLL

THUMP!

CAT-CATS CAN SLEEP WHERE THEY LIKE

It's about 1,400 times more dangerous on the road. 3,000 people around the world die in road crashes every DAY.

On the roads people have died after being crushed in their car by a rolling, half-ton bale of hay.

On the railways people have died from the very first days of steam power. William Huskisson MP was one of the passengers on the train at the opening of the Liverpool to Manchester railway (1830). He stepped out of the carriage when the engine stopped for water and was run over by another engine.

You may feel safe on a nice, slow sea trip. One word. *Titanic*.

So, air travel is safe. But ... and by that, I mean BUT ... it is only safe because brave men and women have taken risks to make flying safer. Some daredevils had to be the first to jump off a high place with wings or test a parachute or fly over water or lift off in a balloon. Some lived. Others didn't. As this is a Horrible Histories book, guess which ones you'll be hearing most about? (No prizes.)

FASTEN YOUR SEAT BELTS

★

PUT YOUR TRAY IN THE UPRIGHT POSITION

★

AND ENJOY THE RIDE!

KITES

THE WOODEN BIRD

R ead this book and learn the secret of how to
fly ... and stay alive. The secret? Invent a flying
machine – then make someone else test it. If it
works, you're a hero, if it fails then someone else
dies. Simple.

2,500 years ago, in China, Mozi the inventor saw a
Chinese farmer who had tied his hat to a string to
keep it from blowing away in a strong wind. Mozi

began to test wind power with kites.

His model kites were made of silk and wood, then he had a bright idea. If a kite were big enough it could lift a human into the air. With help from Lu Ban, a fellow inventor, he built a huge kite he called a 'wooden bird'. The kite pulled with so much power it could lift a person off their feet and into the air. Now, you are asking...

The prisoner may have been asked if he wanted to risk his life on a kite – or lose his life by being executed. Which would you choose?

The imprisoned Prince Yuan Huangtou was one of the prisoners forced to jump off a tower attached to a kite. The others all died. Yuan Huangtou lived ... and was then taken off to be executed.

DID YOU KNOW?

The Chinese also had rockets – not space rockets but the fireworks kind. There is a story that a Chinese inventor attached rockets to his chair, lit the fuses ... and disappeared, never to be seen again.

MADE TO MEASURE

Around 2,200 years ago, the Chinese General Han Xin wanted to measure the distance to the city he planned to attack. He decided to build a tunnel. But that would be no use if the tunnel was too short or too long. Like Goldilocks's porridge it had to be 'just right'. Spies would be shot if they tried to measure the distance.

Then General Han Xin had an idea.

It worked. General Han Xin beat the defences and captured the city.

NOW THAT'S WHAT I CALL AN
ARROW ESCAPE!

DID YOU KNOW?

In the 1600s, traders from Europe went to China and brought the flying gadgets back with them. They reminded the English of a bird of prey – the 'Kite' – so they gave this name to the Chinese flying machine.

JUMPERS

LEGENDARY LEAPERS

In the Greek legend, Daedalus and his son Icarus were imprisoned on an island, which they tried to escape from with wings made from wax. The legend says Icarus flew too close to the sun, melting his wings and so plunged into the sea. But YOU know that the higher you climb in the sky the COLDER it gets. It's a silly myth.

YOU COULD SAY IT WAS A MYTH-TAKE

15

But others throughout history were also inspired by birds in the sky and tried to build their own wings to join the flying flocks.

DID YOU KNOW?

The first animal to fly in an aircraft was a pig named Icarus II. John Moore-Brabazon took Icarus II up in his plane in 1909. It was a joke to prove the saying, 'Pigs might fly'.

FROM PIGSTY TO PIG-SKY

★ **CHOPS AWAY** ★

JUST CALL ME PIGGLES

SPANISH FLEW

Abbas ibn Firnas (810–887AD) was a Spanish inventor. A history book (written 800 years after he died) said...

Abbas ibn Firnas covered himself with feathers, attached a couple of wings to his body and, getting on a high place, flung himself into the air. People who saw him said he flew a good distance, as if he had been a bird, but on landing his back was very much hurt. He did not know that when they land, birds come down upon their tails. He had forgot to make himself one.

– I NEEDED A TAIL ENDING

Reports said Abbas ibn Firnas flew his glider for ten minutes at a time.

A poem written at the time said he was as fast as an ostrich in flight but forgot to be as strong as a vulture. (Ostriches don't fly so it's a bit like saying he was as fast as an Egyptian mummy in flight.)

Maybe the poem should have been written...

There was an inventor in Spain
Who had an enormous great brain.
But when he tried flying
He came close to dying.
And ended up with lots of back pain.

OUCH

HE'S TOO HEAVY, HE'S MY BROTHER

In the 11th century an English monk, Brother Eilmer of Malmesbury, may have read about Abbas ibn Firnas or believed the tale of Icarus. A brother monk told the story of how Eilmer decided to give flying a shot himself.

Eilmer was a wise old man but in his early youth had tried a deed of great daring. He had tied wings to his hands and feet so that he might fly like Icarus. He faced the breeze upon the top of a tower, flew for more than 200 yards. But a strong gust of wind made him fall and break both his legs. He was lame ever after. He used to tell his brothers that he failed because he forgot to give himself a tail.

OUCH

Eilmer also said,

The abbot refused to let Eilmer try it again.

CALLING ALL QUILL SEEKERS

DOES YOUR IDEA HAVE WINGS?
WE'LL HELP YOU GET IT OFF THE GROUND

CHICKENS NEED NOT APPLY

KING BIRDBRAIN

If eagles are the answer, then one man had the right idea.

King Kāvus of Persia had a flying craft made. It was his throne. Four long poles were fastened to it pointing upward. Specially trained eagles were chained to each pole. Pieces of meat were tied at the top of each pole and as the hungry eagles tried to reach the meat they caused the throne to fly.

The craft flew the king all the way to China, where the eagles grew tired and the craft came down. The king survived the crash by some miracle.

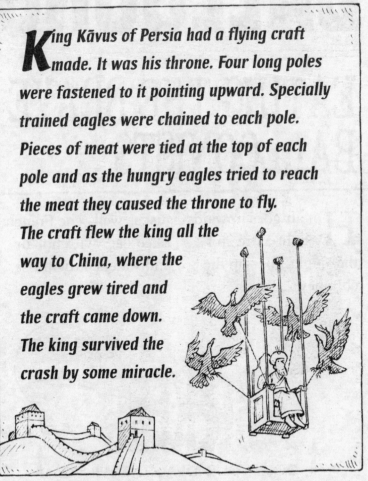

Don't try this at home even if you do have four pet budgies.

BALLOONS

EATING THE BRAVE BALLOONISTS

Hot air goes upwards – light a fire and the smoke goes up the chimney ... which is just as well. The French filled bags with hot air and watched them rise.

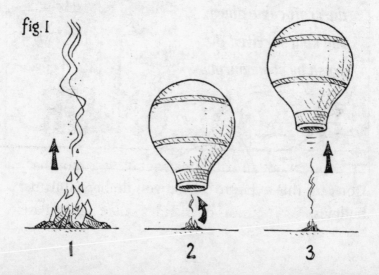

fig. I

1

2

3

ANIMALS AT ALTITUDE

On 19 September 1783, the Montgolfier brothers sent a duck, a sheep and a cockerel up in a hot air balloon. The animals landed safely, though the sheep had kicked the cockerel ... but did they live happily ever after?

There was a feast to celebrate the flight and one writer said the animals were treated like heroes. Another said the animals were eaten.

King Louis XVI of France watched that flight – and probably ate the passengers. Ten years later it was King Louis' turn to be beheaded in the French Revolution. How the duck would have enjoyed that. She'd have quacked up laughing.

FLOATING ON AIR

The next hot air balloonists set off two months later. In November 1783, Jean-François Pilâtre de Rozier and Marquis d'Arlandes sailed across Paris in a Montgolfier balloon, landed and were not eaten. Not even nibbled. They made history.

Two years later, Jean-François Pilâtre de Rozier set off to cross the English Channel in a balloon. His passenger was Pierre Romain. A letter in an English newspaper described what happened:

15 June 1785

Poor Pilârtre de Rozier and a Mons. Romain ascended in the grand balloon, at seven this morning, and made a fine appearance in the ascent, bidding fair for a prosperous voyage to England, but in half an hour, when they were at a great height, and about three miles from the town, the balloon caught fire, and of course fell to the ground. The two intrepid adventurers were dashed to pieces. I was with the bodies in half an hour and never saw anything so shocking.

I examined the bodies but do not find anything broke above the middle, so that they must have come down perpendicularly, but their legs and thighs were broke in many places. I shook hands with de Rozier, almost the last person in his lifetime; he was a fine young fellow, and thought for several days past had a presentiment of his untimely end in his countenance...

Mr Jean-François Pilâtre de Rozier was a teacher. He once wanted to prove that hydrogen burned fiercely. He gulped a large mouthful of hydrogen and blew it across a flame – it burned. And so did his eyebrows.

HORRIBLE HISTORIES HEALTH WARNING:

Do NOT try this yourself in your school chemistry lesson. Ask your teacher to do it. It is a good test. A test to see how daft your teacher is.

BIT DAFT   DAFT   VERY DAFT   HALF-BAKED

Now, he KNEW hydrogen burned but he powered his balloon with a mix of hydrogen AND hot air (from a burner.) When his balloon crashed the burner set fire to the hydrogen and Mr de Rozier became Mr de Roasted.

He may have died but he is famous because he was the first person to die in an air crash.

> DO YOU MIND? I WAS FAMOUS FOR THE FIRST UNTETHERED BALLOON FLIGHT, TOO. SO THAT'S DYING *AND* FLYING

UP AGAINST IT

Mr de Rozier wanted to be the first person to fly across the English Channel. He was never going to be that. Two men had already done it together ... even though they hated one another. And you will not BELIEVE what trick they used to make their balloon lighter. (But don't worry, I'll tell you.) Here is their terrifying tale. See if you can guess what happened next...

1. Jean-Pierre Blanchard was French and had flown balloons but had no money. John Jeffries was an American (living in England) and he had money and wanted to be the

first person to fly across the English Channel in a balloon. With Blanchard's skill and Jeffries' money they could do it together except ... **what?**

2. Blanchard wanted to do it alone and get all the glory. In January 1785, he tried to stop Jeffries getting into the balloon as it was ready to take off from Dover. He said the balloon was too heavy and Jeffries could not go. And it was heavy because ... **why?**

3. Blanchard was wearing a belt filled with lead weights. Jeffries discovered this and the belt was thrown out. They set off in a gentle breeze. The weather was calm, but the flight wasn't because ... **why?**

4. The two men started arguing. Jeffries tore Blanchard's French flag off the balloon and Blanchard ripped off Jeffries flag. The flags ended up in the sea and the men almost did too. This would have been a tragedy because ... **why?**

5. Neither man could swim. Halfway across the Channel they started to lose height. They threw anything out they didn't need. France came in sight, but they still needed to lose weight. They threw the only thing left into the sea ... **what?**

6. They took off all their clothes (except their underpants) and threw them into the sea. Still they slipped towards the icy waters. That's when Jeffries came up with an idea. There was something they could do to make themselves lighter. He told Blanchard they should ... **what?**

7. Pee over the side of the basket. (I told you that you wouldn't believe it.) They reached the shores of France but something unexpected happened ... **what?**

8. The balloon was lifted into the sky again by warm air from the land. They had thrown away the ropes and anchors that would have let them land safely. They sailed on at treetop height for ten more miles until ... **what?**

9. Jeffries was able to grab the top branches of a tall tree. This slowed them down enough to let gas escape and the balloon come down safely. They returned the ten miles to the coast in a carriage. They were greeted as heroes, but not in their underpants because ... **why?**

10. Local people had given them clothes. Jeffries had saved one thing from being thrown into the Channel. It was a letter that he had stuffed into his underpants. The first ever airmail letter was delivered by a smarty pants.

IT'S A FIRST CLASS TALE OF A MALE THAT SAVED THE MAIL

LADIES WHO LAUNCH

The warbling woman

A year before de Rozier crashed, the first women to fly took to the air in France. Countess of Montalembert, the Countess of Podenas and Miss de Lagarde went up in a balloon over Paris, in 1784. The balloon stayed fastened to ropes so they didn't fly free.

That was left to Élisabeth Thible who flew over Lyon in France untethered. But it wasn't just a sight worth seeing. It was a sight worth listening to. Miss Thible sang songs from popular operas to entertain King Gustav III of Sweden.

SHE CERTAINLY HITS THE HIGH NOTES. *HIGH* NOTES, GEDDIT?

More daring was Jeanne Geneviève Labrosse who was the first woman to jump from a balloon with a parachute. She leaped from 900 m in 1799 and survived!

Sizzling Sophie

Sophie married Jean-Pierre Blanchard, the famous French hot air balloonist. He made a lot of money ... but he spent it very quickly. Sophie took to the air to stop them from starving.

A woman balloonist was unusual, and she was very popular. She flew for Emperor Napoleon and for King Louis XVIII and her most spectacular trick was to light fireworks from her balloon basket then float them down on little parachutes. But she used balloons filled with hydrogen, not hot air, and hydrogen explodes when it touches a flame.

For her 59th flight she dressed in a white dress and a hat made of ostrich feathers to put on one of her fireworks shows. The wind was gusty and the people who were there said she looked worried.

Sophie soared into the sky and lit a mixture called Bengal fire. It burned fiercely and would light up the balloon so the crowds could see it in the sky.

That evening, a spark set fire to the hydrogen

in the balloon. As the balloon burned the crowds cheered. They thought it was part of the show. The balloon fell and Sophie was tipped out into the streets below.

Sophie Blanchard had two 'Famous Firsts'. The good news? She was the first woman to pilot her own balloon when she took off from a monastery garden in Toulouse, France, in 1799.

AND THE BAD NEWS? I BECAME THE FIRST WOMAN TO DIE IN AN AIR ACCIDENT WHEN MY BALLOON CAUGHT FIRE. FLYING *AND* DYING

Her gravestone reads:

> # A victim of her art and her courage.

DRIVING FORCE

The French balloonists learned to steer their balloons. But Henri Giffard was the first person to power a balloon and steer it. In 1852, Henri invented the first powered airship with a steam engine that drove a propeller.

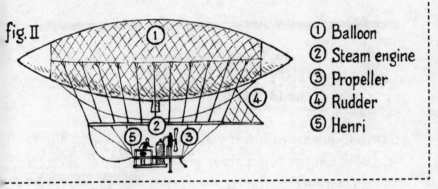

fig. II

① Balloon
② Steam engine
③ Propeller
④ Rudder
⑤ Henri

He went over 25 km from Paris to the town of Trappes with the wind behind him. The wind was too strong to allow him to fly against it, so he was unable to return to the start. But he was able to make turns and circles, showing that a powered airship could be steered and could fly anywhere on a calm day.

Henri worked on the French railways and made very little money. The cost of building his first airship left him poor. His inventions started to make him money and he used it to build a second airship. That didn't work so well, and it crashed.

DID YOU KNOW?

The famous Eiffel Tower was built in 1889. On the tower there are 72 names stamped ... the names of the 72 people who made France great. Henri Giffard's name is there.

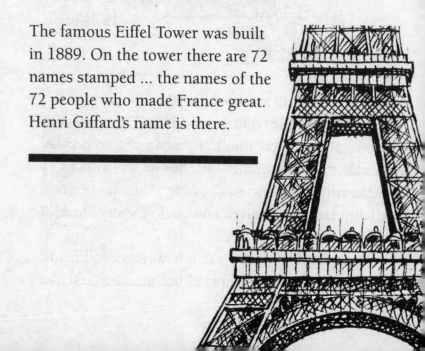

DUCKING AND DIVING

Even after flying machines were invented, there was still a use for balloons. In the Second World War (1939–1945) Britain was attacked by enemy bombers. It was a time known as The Blitz.

The Blitzed Brits were especially afraid of dive bombers. These aeroplanes swooped low to drop their bombs. To stop this sort of bombing 'barrage balloons' were invented.

These were huge, silvery balloons, each as big as a house. They were filled with gas and floated over towns, held down by heavy steel cables. Dive bombers were torn apart by these cables.

Many people felt safe under the cover of these silver cigar shaped balloons.

One boy described them:

But the barrage balloons also caused some problems…

• Sometimes the cables on a balloon snapped and the balloon floated away.

• A balloon could catch fire – from a lightning strike or enemy plane attack. Then it could come down on the houses below.

• A loose balloon trailed its wires. If they caught overhead power cables, they could leave a town without power for many hours.

GLIDERS

BOY RACERS

George Cayley (1773–1857) was British. He saw other inventors try to make flapping wings that failed to fly. He did experiments on the shape of the wings and found the best. He made flying models first. Then in 1849 he built a full-sized glider. Would YOU offer to be fastened into it and launched off the side of a hill? Would YOU want to be a pilot?

AHARRRR, ME HEARTIES

No, I said a pilot. You'd be daft to risk your life.

Remember the secret of safe experiments? (Have you been paying attention?) Yes. Let someone else be the first to try it. Cayley sent one of his servants into the air in his glider. It was a 10-year-old serving boy. He had a choice: get in ... or get the sack and starve to death. Which would you choose?

Cayley's invention was called a 'heavier-than-air' machine even though it was actually the world's first aeroplane.

★ **THE WORLD'S FIRST AEROPLANE** ★

MORE LIKE THE WORLD'S FIRST FLYING BOAT

A heavier-than-air machine

The boy was the first person in history to make a flight in an aeroplane. He should be famous. Is he? No. We don't even know his name.

WELL DONE, WHATEVER YOUR NAME IS

But we DO know the name of an early balloon boy. Young Edward Warren was just 13 when he became the first person to take part in a US balloon flight.

A newspaper reported:

The Baltimore Gazette
28 Aug 1784

Edward Warren, a youth of 13 years of age, was fastened into the balloon and it soon went out of sight. It was in the air near two hours and the weather being exceedingly calm. It came down about two miles from Baltimore, amidst many cheering people. They were generous with their money for the boy and the courage he had shown.

Then Caley tried to find a way to power the flight. He used gunpowder – a sort of jet-engine. You can bet that went with a bang.

IT WAS JUST A FLASH IN THE PAN

George Cayley built a glider with three wings in 1853. Now it was time to fly an adult. Would Cayley himself test it? Don't be silly. He sent his coach driver. The glider crashed and the man was hurt. Famous, but battered like a chip shop cod.

DID YOU KNOW?

In 1910, Horatio Barber built the first British powered aircraft to fly. His first effort failed. Just like Cayley, Barber chose his car driver – chauffeur – as the test pilot. The chauffeur, Bertie Woodrow, had never flown an aeroplane before, but the brilliant Barber said…

Bertie tried to take off from Larkhill near
Stonehenge ... but failed and narrowly missed
demolishing the ancient stones. In 1912, one
of Barber's aeroplanes crashed to the west of
Stonehenge and killed the two fliers.

MOUNTAIN GLIDES

Otto Lilienthal was the most successful glider
builder and pilot. He needed a hill to fly from, so

he built one – a mound of earth about 15 metres high.

He made 2,000 flights in around 16 different gliders. Only one failed. The last one. In 1896 his glider stalled and he crashed to the ground from 15 metres in the air. He broke his neck and died the next day. His last words were...

SACRIFICES MUST BE MADE

A Briton who died trying was Percy Pilcher. Percy flew one of Lilienthal's gliders off the mound then went home to Britain to build his own.

He built a glider called *The Bat* in 1895. His sister helped stitch the wings and they made the world record glide of 250 metres.

THE BAT

Percy was planning a glider that would have a motor – a powered flying machine at last. Unfortunately, the engine broke down just before he planned to make the historic flight. He was desperate for money and the people with money had come to watch. He set off in his glider, *The Hawk*, instead.

It was a stormy day, the tail snapped off *The Hawk*, and he fell 10 metres to the ground. He died two days later.

★ SEE ★

- The original **The Hawk** has survived and is in the National Museums Scotland in Edinburgh.
- A full-size model of **The Bat** can be seen at the Riverside Museum, Glasgow.

THE HAWK

PARACHUTES

If you head off to sea in a boat, you plan in case you start to sink ... or you lose power when a mermaid gets tangled in your propeller, or you need to go ashore to pick a coconut on a desert island. How do you prepare? You take a smaller boat with you. A lifeboat.

And what if you are in an aeroplane and you hit problems? (A mermaid tangled in your propeller, maybe?) Then you need a way to escape safely. You need a parachute.

JUST IN CASE I LAND ON WATER

Parachutes have saved thousands of lives. But some brave pioneers had to TEST the things to see if they worked. And if they didn't work then the pioneers went splat. A popular children's song told the horrible story long before Horrible Histories books were invented. (Children are just so cruel, aren't they?)

He Jumped Without A Parachute

(To the tune of 'John Brown's Body')

He jumped without a parachute from twenty
thousand feet
He jumped without a parachute from twenty
thousand feet
He jumped without a parachute from twenty
thousand feet
And he ain't gonna jump no more

CHORUS: Glory, glory what a hell of a way to die
Glory, glory what a hell of a way to die
Glory, glory what a hell of a way to die
And he ain't gonna jump no more

Verse 2: He landed on the pavement like a lump
of strawberry jam
He landed on the pavement like a lump
of strawberry jam

He landed on the pavement like a lump
of strawberry jam

Verse 3: They put him in a matchbox, and they sent
him home to mum

Verse 4: She put him on the table when the Vicar
came to tea

Verse 5: The Vicar spread him on some toast and
said what lovely jam

Chorus: Glory, glory what a hell of a way to die
Suspended by your braces when you don't know how
to fly
Glory, glory what a hell of a way to die
And he ain't gonna jump no more

HIGH JUMPERS

Some were brave, some were reckless, and some were just plain stupid. Here are the top ten jumpers.

1 Lamb Chop.

Jean Pierre Blanchard (the first man to balloon across the English Channel) made money by showing how parachutes worked. He threw animals out of his balloon and the public loved to see them land safely. But the public soon went off the spectacle when a dog and a sheep died in puddles of blood.

HORRIBLE HISTORIES NOTE:

These charming Horrible Histories books would NEVER, never, ever put in a joke like this ...

OH LOOK. A WOOLLY JUMPER

Never, EVER.

Jean-Pierre Blanchard had a heart attack while flying a balloon. He fell 15 metres out of the basket and died a year later. Sheep and dogs everywhere must have been pleased.

2 Shop till you drop.

Franz Reichelt was an Austrian tailor who owned a dressmaking shop in the middle of Paris. He had moved to France in 1898 and did well as a dressmaker – he was a cut above the rest. At some point, he got a passion for flying but he wasn't cut out for it. He was sure he could invent a parachute that pilots could wear.

His b-i-g idea was the 'parachute suit'. They were fixed parachutes that were held open by wood, but they took up a lot of room. He tried his parachute suit from about 10 metres ... and broke his leg. He kept trying and thought if he jumped from somewhere higher the parachute suit would catch the air and let him float down.

On 4 February 1912, Franz Reichelt arrived at the Eiffel Tower, dressed in his suit strutting about for cameras of the press. His friends thought he'd throw a dummy off the Tower to test it. He didn't. As the cameras rolled he stood on a chair to reach the top of the fence and threw himself off.

Warwickshire County Council

Warwickshire
County Council

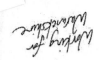

Working for Warwickshire

LEA 04/21

This item is to be returned or renewed before the latest date above. It may be borrowed for a further period if not in demand. **To renew your books:**

- **Phone the 24/7 Renewal Line 01926 499273 or**
- **Visit www.warwickshire.gov.uk/libraries**

Discover • Imagine • Learn • *with libraries*

It was a short, fast trip to the ground as the parachute didn't open.

What Franz didn't know was that just two days prior to his jump, an American parachutist, Frederick R. Law, had made a successful jump from the Statue of Liberty with a wearable parachute. Franz the dressmaker wouldn't have been a Famous First even if he'd survived.

I FELL TOWER

3 Cross my art and hope to die.

In July 1837, a seriously weird artist, Robert Cocking, jumped from under a hot air balloon to test a parachute. Robert was 61 years old that year – quite a wrinklie at that time. His parachute looked like an umbrella when blown inside out.

Robert had a drink of wine, took off his coat and climbed into the basket under the parachute. A hot air balloon carried the whole thing 1.5 km into the air over London. Brave Bob pulled a rope and let the parachute go. His last words were called up to the balloon pilots …

I never felt more comfortable or more delighted in my life. Well, now I think I shall leave you. Good night, Spencer; Good night, Green.

He jumped and fell towards Greenwich in London. He fell very fast. The stitching that held the parachute was a bit feeble. The parachute

OH SILLY ME … I FORGOT TO ADD THE WEIGHT OF THE PARACHUTE. ANOTHER 110 KILOS

was made to carry his weight – 90 kg. Maybe that's when he remembered...

The basket fell off and Robert was smashed on the ground like a hedgehog on a motorway.

4. The pain in Spain.

Abbas ibn Firnas was one of the first fliers. He was also the first to try a parachute. In the year 852AD, when he jumped off the minaret of the Great Mosque of Cordoba in Spain.

Reports say he used canvas for the parachute. He went down quickly and ended up with several broken bones after a rough landing. Still, he was sure it would work and was the Famous First – well, the first to live to tell his story. If it's true, then he made the first parachute jump in history.

Someone else who jumped from the tower of a mosque was Abu al-Nasr Ismael Al-Johari, who lived around 1,000AD in Turkistan. A historian wrote...

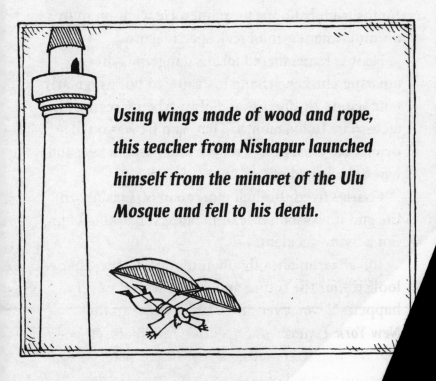

Using wings made of wood and rope, this teacher from Nishapur launched himself from the minaret of the Ulu Mosque and fell to his death.

You will notice he was a teacher.

THE 'CRAZY MAN OF THE AIR'

Charles 'Daredevil' Hamilton (1885–1914) was an American flier known as the 'crazy man of the air'. He started at the age of 18 doing parachute jumps from balloons for money. He went on to fly around America and break speed records.

He was remembered for his dangerous dives, amazing crashes, having his battered body regularly patched up by doctors and always being seen with a cigarette in his mouth. They said he was often drunk. He once flew – very drunk – into a lake and had to be fished out.

Charles lived through more than 60 crashes. In the end it was a disease of the lungs that killed him, not a flying accident.

Today aeroplanes fly on autopilot. Crazy Charles ~ked into the future and said it would never ~n. Never, ever. In 1910 he wrote in the ~ Times...

> *I don't think there will ever be an automatic aeroplane. Such a machine would drive the plane into headwinds and it would be hopelessly ripped to pieces. There will be automatic planes when they make a pair of eyes for a car that will let it drive down the street without hitting anything.*

Autopilot planes and driverless cars? If Charlie had seen them today, he'd have thought he was drunk ... again.

MAKE YOUR OWN PARACHUTE

You can see how a parachute works without jumping out of a hot air balloon or off the Eiffel Tower and killing yourself. (And NO ... you cannot throw your teacher off the school roof either. They could make a horrible hole in the playground.)

Instead, you can make a model to see how it works.

WHAT YOU'LL NEED:

• a plastic bag or light material

Ask an adult for help

• scissors

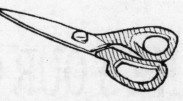

• string

• a small object to act as the weight - a little action figure or doll would be perfect

I've got a bad feeling about this

INSTRUCTIONS:

STEP ONE: cut out a large square from your plastic bag or material. Trim the edges so it looks like an octagon (an eight-sided shape).

STEP TWO: cut a small hole near the edge of the 8 points of the octagon.

STEP THREE: attach 8 pieces of string of the same length to each of the holes. Tie the pieces of string to the object you are using as a weight.

STEP FOUR: use a chair or find a high spot to drop your parachute and test how well it worked, remember that you want it to drop as slowly as possible.

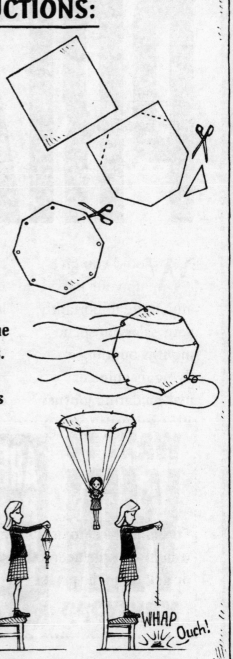

WHAP
Ouch!

PRIZES

Would you give up your job and, more importantly, your salary to spend months building a flying machine or make a daring journey? Maybe not. But what if someone offered a lot of money? Prizes have tempted a lot of inventors to go hungry, risk their lives ... and even lose their lives.

WANT TO WIN MONEY???

ARE YOU DARING? Not Afraid of Heights? Then Enter NOW!

★ **WARNING:** Pilots may die. ★
Terms and Conditions apply

A) SANTOS-DUMONT

In 1900, a rich Frenchman offered the Deutsch prize of 100,000 francs to any airship flier who could circle the Eiffel Tower in Paris.

To win the money, the airship had to take off from the nearby town of Saint-Cloud, fly to Paris, circle the tower, and fly back to Saint-Cloud. Seven miles in under 30 minutes.

A number of pilots tried for the prize and failed. Alberto Santos-Dumont did not care about the money because he was from a family of rich coffee producers. (Alberto was from Brazil. He came to France on a ship, not a balloon.)

Alberto wanted to show how well his new balloons could fly.

DO NOT CALL THEM BALLOONS, PLEASE. MY FLYING MACHINES CAN BE STEERED AND THEY ARE CALLED 'DIRIGIBLES'

He tried for the prize once and failed, as all the others had. He lived through a couple of crashes. But on 19 October 1901, he tried again and won.

His Dirigible Number 6 came from Saint-Cloud, flew in a little circle around the Eiffel Tower and made it back to Saint-Cloud in exactly 29 and a half minutes.

Alberto went to his friend, Louis Cartier, to make him a wristwatch. Between them they came up with an idea that changed timekeeping. (And the Cartier company are STILL making Santos-Dumont wristwatches over a hundred years later.)

As for the prize, Alberto said...

Nice man. He became famous and enjoyed his life in Paris. He would float his dirigible along Paris streets, at rooftop level, and sometimes land at a cafe for lunch.

He set off for America to win another prize. But when his airship was unpacked from the boat it had been wrecked.

Alberto went on to make heavier-than-air machines before he retired to Brazil in 1924.

The idea of his machines being used to kill people upset him terribly. He took his own life.

A sad end to a rare inventor who worked with both balloons and heavier-than-air machines.

B) LOUIS BLERIOT ENGLISH CHANNEL 25 JULY 1909

First flight across water

Human beings have come up with some brilliant inventions. But sooner or later someone really brave has to try them out to see if they are safe for the rest of us.

Louis Bleriot is famous for being the first person to fly across water. He flew from France to England and his name went down in history. It was the most famous French landing since William the Conqueror landed at Hastings in 1066. But Bleriot should NOT have won the race to be first. He was just plain lucky...

DID YOU KNOW?

I WAS A REAL BRIGHT SPARK

Bleriot was an engineer who had made his fortune inventing gas headlamps for cars.

• He then spent his money in cracking the problem of flight. As early as 1900 he had built an ornithopter – an aircraft that flies by flapping its wings.

THAT IDEA DIDN'T GET OFF THE GROUND... NOO ... *REALLY DIDN'T GET OFF THE GROUND*

• He went on building dangerous machines. At last, he got the Bleriot V off the ground, but it crashed easily. A bit of a nuisance. Just as he finished building the Bleriot XI the *Daily Mail* newspaper announced a contest.

★ **£1,000** ★

★ **PRIZE** ★

FOR THE FIRST PILOT TO FLY ACROSS THE ENGLISH CHANNEL

• Bleriot needed the money, but he had a great rival for that prize. Hubert Latham was a filthy-rich Frenchman with an English grandfather. He flew an Antoinette plane using an engine from a motor yacht. The Antoinette broke records and won prizes in Europe and America – it was top favourite to win the *Mail's* money.

• Latham set off a week before Bleriot was ready. But that yacht engine failed, and Latham became the first man to make a successful landing at sea. The rescuers found him sitting calmly in his plane, smoking a cigarette. He was just 6 miles short of the English coast.

• Bleriot had a second chance. Latham had a new machine ready. He told Bleriot...

But disaster struck. As Bleriot was testing his XI machine a fuel line split, a fire broke out and his foot was burned. He bravely agreed to carry on. It was his last chance. At first light, Bleriot soared into history as he flew the 22 miles in 37 minutes. Rain on the engine, strong crosswinds and mist failed to beat him. He was a hero of history around the world.

What happened to Latham? you cry. If I tell you, you won't believe it. Have a guess...

a) He crashed into the sea ... again

b) He crashed into a seagull and smashed his propeller. (The seagull was a bit smashed too.)

c) His servant forgot to set the alarm clock, so Latham was still asleep when dawn broke.

Answer: (c) Latham overslept. He wasn't ready to fly at dawn. That's how history is made.

64

★ SEE ★

Louis Bleriot Memorial, Northfall Meadow, Dover Castle, Kent. The outline of his aircraft is laid out in stone in the turf and marks his landing spot on the cliffs above Dover.

See Bleriot's Famous First plane controls in the Science Museum, London as well as a flying model.

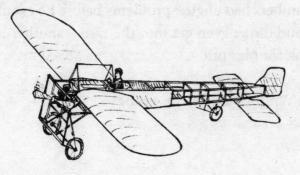

FAST FACTS

• The Wright Brothers in the USA had already flown but were too scared to fly over water.

• Count Charles de Lambert bought a plane from Wilbur Wright to win the Cross-Channel prize.

• Wilbur had been offered an extra £1,500 if he made the flight across the water himself.

• Brother Orville Wright told Wilbur not to try it. Orville said they were going to make lots of money from selling aeroplanes. They didn't need to risk their lives flying over water.

• Lambert had engine problems before he even set off and didn't even get into the race – another lucky break for Bleriot.

The Wright plane went wrong.

C) ALCOCK AND BROWN

In 1913, the *Daily Mail* first offered a prize of £10,000 for the first non-stop flight across the

Atlantic Ocean. At that time there were no flying machines that could get near that distance. Their money was safe.

Then along came the First World War and the countries at war started building bombers that flew as far as possible to drop bombs on enemy towns.

The British had the Vickers Vimy bomber. In 1919 British fliers John Alcock and Arthur Brown were able to fly it from Newfoundland to County Galway in Ireland.

DID YOU KNOW?

1 Both Alcock and Brown had been pilots in the First World War and both had crashed and become prisoners of war.

2 It was a race against time to win the prize. Other fliers were testing their aircraft so Alcock and Brown set off in a hurry. They almost crashed at the start as the heavy plane struggled to climb over trees at the end of the runway.

3 There was no cover over the cockpit. Even though it was June they suffered snow and ice as well as a thick fog that meant they had to blind-fly almost the entire way.

4 The aircraft's exhaust pipe burst and made a noise so loud they could barely hear one another. The electrics failed so they had no radio and no heating. *Brrrrr*.

5 After 16 hours of flying they reached Galway to the west of Ireland. They thought they saw a nice green field to land. It turned out to be a nice green bog. Their plane stuck, nose first, in the mud and was damaged. Alcock and Brown lived and were heroes.

After they landed, they were the coolest men in Ireland. As they travelled to Clifden town, on a stagecoach, they said ...

THAT IS THE WAY TO FLY THE ATLANTIC

IF WE HAVE A SHAVE AND A BATH WE SHOULD BE ALL RIGHT

Alcock and Brown needed all the luck they could get. John Alcock took a lucky black toy cat called Lucky Jim. Brown also had a lucky toy cat which he called Twinkletoes… Well, it's nice to have a bit of company.

As well as these toy cats, they also had a lucky white heather flower and a horseshoe underneath Alcock's seat in the aircraft for luck.

Arthur Brown lived on to see a second world war but a few months after crossing the Atlantic, John Alcock set off for the Paris air show. His plane crashed and he died.

★ **SEE** ★

There is a statue to Alcock and Brown at Heathrow Airport, London.

A monument stands where they landed in Errislannan, Co Galway, West Ireland.

Lucky cat Twinkletoes is now at the RAF Museum, Cosford.

The Science Museum, London has the actual Vickers Vimy aircraft that Alcock and Brown flew.

A Vickers Vimy replica can be seen at the Brooklands Museum, Weybridge, Surrey.

D)CHARLES LINDBERGH

Alcock and Brown showed it was possible to cross the Atlantic on an aircraft. But a greater prize was to be the first person to fly ALONE across the Atlantic Ocean from the USA to Europe.

A New York hotel keeper, Raymond Orteig, offered a $25,000 prize for the first person to fly alone – non-stop – across the Atlantic Ocean. The prize was so great, several fliers died trying.

In 1926, Frenchman René Fonck crashed on take-off from New York. All the extra fuel made it too heavy. In the First World War he'd shot down at least 75 enemy planes. Fonck survived the crash but two people were killed.

NOW HE'S KILLED 76

MAKE THAT 77

Navy pilots Noel Davis and Stanton H. Wooster were killed in Virginia in 1927, while testing their Atlantic flier.

The same year, French war heroes Charles Nungesser and François Coli left Paris on their Levasseur PL, nicknamed "L'Oiseau Blanc". They disappeared somewhere in the Atlantic after being seen crossing the west coast of Ireland.

Charles Lindbergh (1902–1974) was an American flying postman and inventor. Lindbergh said he hated the men and women who flew stunt planes to entertain people. But Lindbergh started out as an assistant to stunt flier Errold Bahl. As a special treat for Bahl's audiences, Lindbergh climbed out on to the wing of the plane to wave to the crowds below. This became known as 'wing-walking.'

Then, at the age of 25 in 1927, Lindbergh became world famous by making the non-stop flight from New York to Paris and winning the Orteig Prize.

Lindbergh became the most famous man in America. The trouble with being famous is you attract criminals who want a share of your money. In 1932, his infant son was kidnapped and Lindbergh paid a huge ransom of $50,000. But the child was found dead in some woods near his home in what the Americans called the 'crime of the century' and the 'biggest story since Jesus rose from the dead'.

A German carpenter living in America, Richard Hauptmann, was arrested after he paid for petrol with some of the ransom cash. Some people believe Hauptmann was innocent, but it didn't really matter in the end.

It seems the Americans wanted someone to pay for the crime against their hero Lindbergh.

Not many of the prize winners ended happy ever after.

POWERED FLIGHT

Of all the Famous Firsts, the greatest one is this one: who made the first powered flight? Most people say it was brothers Orville and Wilbur Wright in the USA in 1903.

Not everyone agrees.

Apart from birds (and pterodactyls) which human made the first powered flight? Well, it depends who you believe.

WILBUR AND ORVILLE WRIGHT

In 1901, the Wright brothers were fed up with flying. Their gliders didn't fly as far as they hoped and most of the landings were crash landings.

Wilbur probably did all the gliding until 1902. He was the big brother and didn't want young Orville to get hurt. He probably worried what their dad, Milton, would say if Orville got injured.

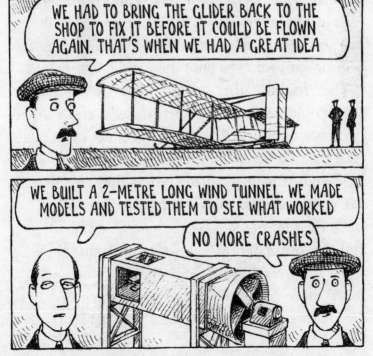

WE HAD TO BRING THE GLIDER BACK TO THE SHOP TO FIX IT BEFORE IT COULD BE FLOWN AGAIN. THAT'S WHEN WE HAD A GREAT IDEA

WE BUILT A 2-METRE LONG WIND TUNNEL. WE MADE MODELS AND TESTED THEM TO SEE WHAT WORKED

NO MORE CRASHES

They found a model that worked well and built a full-sized plane. It was flown as a kite at first – held down by ropes. It needed to fly with the weight of a pilot, of course. What did the Wright Brothers use for weight? A boy from the nearby town. Would YOU like that job?

They looked for a light petrol engine, but no factories could give them what they wanted. Instead one of the workers in their own workshop, Charlie Taylor, built them a motor. (The Wright Brothers are famous for ever but Charlie is forgotten.)

On 17 December 1903, Orville flew 37 metres – the length of four buses. Humans had made the first ever powered flight. Orville would have another Famous First just five years later. The first person ever killed in a powered aeroplane crash was Lieutenant Thomas Selfridge in 1908. The pilot was Orville Wright.

The Wrights' father, Milton, made them promise they would never fly together in case a crash wiped them both out. In 1910, he let them do it just once. And then Dad climbed into the plane. He was 81 years old. Was he terrified? No, as they rose to over 100 metres the old man cried...

Wilbur died from typhoid in 1912 – he probably ate some bad fish.

But Orville lived on until 1948, so he saw two world wars, The Blitz, the hydrogen bomb the US dropped on Hiroshima, Japan, and planes that flew faster than the speed of sound. He was sad about the bombings and said…

We hoped we had invented something that would bring lasting peace to the earth. But we were wrong… No, I don't have any regrets about my part in inventing the aeroplane. Though no one could deplore more than I do the destruction it has caused.

The Wright Brothers were great pioneers, but other people claimed that brothers were NOT the first to fly a powered plane.

★ **SEE** ★

A model of the Wright Brothers' Famous First plane in the Science Museum, London.

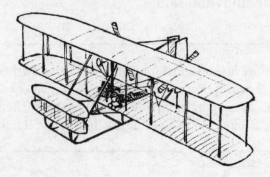

RICHARD PEARSE

Richard Pearse (1877–1953) was a New Zealand farmer and inventor. He didn't say he made the first powered aeroplane ... someone else said it for him.

Richard DID have some amazing ideas:

• a bicycle that was powered by pedals that went up and down instead of around

• tyres that could be pumped up while you are still riding

• an aeroplane whose propeller could be moved from the front to the top and make it a helicopter

• a machine for planting potatoes and another for threading needles

An eight-year-old boy, Robert Gibson, said that he and his friends had seen Pearse fly in March 1903 – more than eight months before the Wright Brothers. Pearse fitted a petrol engine on to his plane and took it on to a hillside.

79

But Richard Pearse NEVER said he beat the Wright Brothers. They had the power to take off. Richard started with a glide and had little control. A brave and clever man but not the first to fly a powered aeroplane.

GUSTAVE'S GRAB FOR GLORY

Gustave Whitehead (1874–1927) said he made a powered flight over two years before the Wright Brothers' first flight. His letters to newspapers told of his successful flights. There was no proof that he actually made them.

WAS HIS STORY LIKE A BALLOON...

FULL OF HOT AIR?

When Gustave was a boy, he studied flying. He made parachutes made of tissue paper and watched birds close up. When he was 13, he jumped from a roof attached to a pair of cloth wings. (He lived but don't go trying that at home with your parents' tablecloth.)

He made his first aeroplane in 1901. He said it flew but there are no photos. One person said he watched Gustave take to the air.

Gustave made his last aeroplane in 1908 – it did not fly. He went on to build helicopters – which also did not fly.

Then, in 1935, a magazine article said that:

Gustave flew a heavier-than-air aircraft in 1901

Of course, the magazine said that eight years after Gustave had died and it has caused arguments ever since.

Gustave Whitehead's steam-driven model had carried him and his assistant a distance of almost a mile. Firemen helped them to start the machine, while the assistant fed charcoal to the flame which heated water in the ordinary kitchen boiler which they were using. They went onward and upward, steered by Gustave Whitehead at the controls in the front, and went far further than they had planned.

Hmmmm. A steam engine is a heavy thing. Picture it: a flier at the front with a fireman stoking the fire under the boiler.

A great story and a wonderful picture. But is it true? You make up your own mind.

THE FIRST WORLD WAR

RACE AGAINST TIME

By 1914, aeroplanes were slowly getting better. Safer and faster and flying further. Then, suddenly, they started to get a lot better in just a few short years. What happened? War happened.

The First World War began between Britain, France and their friends against Germany and their friends.

Just like the Chinese General Han Xin over two thousand years before, the soldiers on both sides wanted to know what was happening on the other side.

Aeroplanes with a pilot and a cameraman (an 'observer') could fly over the heads of the enemy and see what they were up to.

Neither side wanted that so each side had teams of pilots who would try to shoot down the enemy camera planes. These 'fighter' planes had to get faster and stronger and the plane-makers had to work faster than they ever had before.

It was a life and death race.

BOUNCING BULLETS

War planes began to carry machine guns; the pilot aimed his plane at the enemy and pulled the trigger. But there was a danger that the bullets would then hit his own propeller and shatter it. In time engineers invented a 'timing gear' so the bullets could only fire into the gaps between the turning propeller. The British invented it. The Germans copied it. Which side was the first to shoot down the enemy using timing gear? The Germans, of course.

But how did the first machine guns – before timing gear – fire forward through the propeller? If you were an Allied inventor, what simple solution could you come up with?

Answer:

The propellers were covered with sheets of steel. If a machine gun bullet happened to hit the propeller then it bounced off.

Great idea and it worked. For a month or two the German airmen were terrified and puzzled by the British fighter planes. Finally, they captured one, saw how it was done and copied it.

The trouble is there was no way of telling where the bullet would end up if it hit the steel propeller. It could bounce back and smash into the pilot's own engine, if he was unlucky – or bounce back and hit him between the eyes if he was really, really unlucky.

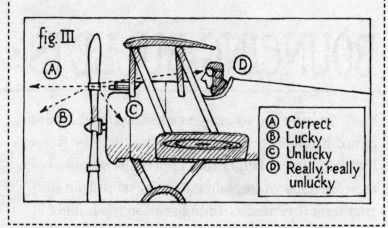

fig. III

Ⓐ Correct
Ⓑ Lucky
Ⓒ Unlucky
Ⓓ Really really unlucky

GAS BAG GRIEF

Count Ferdinand Zeppelin, a German army officer, started building airships in 1897. The German army started using them in 1909. At the start of the First World War the German Army had seven Zeppelins. They sent them over Britain to bomb their British enemies in their homes.

The first Zeppelin raid on London was on 31 May 1915. The attack killed 28 people and injured 60 more. But the huge airships could be shot down by fighter planes.

On 24 September 1916, Zeppelin L-33 was under the command of Captain Alois Bocker. It was shot at and they were forced to land near New Hall Cottages, Little Wigborough.

Bocker then did an odd thing – he knocked on the doors of the cottages...

But the fire didn't destroy the Zeppelin and the British balloon builders learned a lot from the wreck.

Bocker marched his men towards Colchester but he was met by Constable Charles Smith. One man against a crew of enemy airmen.

With the help of the Special Constables in the village, the German airmen were led towards Mersea Island where the army took them prisoner. From that day on, Charles Smith was known as 'Zepp' Smith. He died in 1977 at the age of 94.

There were a total of 51 German Zeppelin raids on Britain in which 5,806 bombs were dropped, killing 557 people and injuring 1,358. 115 Zeppelins were used during the First World War but 77 were shot down and many more were lost in accidents.

DAFT DORA

The Zeppelin raids scared the people. The government came up with new rules to protect them. They came up with DORA. Who was DORA? DORA was Britain's 'Defence Of the Realm Act'.

The people of Britain had to live by DORA's rules. But what were the rules? Here are some strange regulations. But which are real DORA rules and which are real daft rules?

Defence of the Realm Act

YOU MUST NOT...

1 loiter under a railway bridge.

2 send a letter overseas written in invisible ink.

3 fly a kite that could be used for signalling.

4 speak in a foreign language on the telephone.

One rule which upset children was one that said,

YOU MUST **NOT** KEEP FRAGMENTS OF ZEPPELINS OR BOMBS AS SOUVENIRS

Still, children hunted for these and ignored the law.
  The people who wrote DORA were sure
Zeppelins could see and hear the tiniest sound or
light from people in the streets. When the airmen
heard or saw something, they would drop a bomb.

That's why DORA rules said that was against the law to...

A) RING CHURCH BELLS AFTER SUNDOWN.

B) WHISTLE IN THE STREET AFTER 10 P.M. FOR A TAXI.

C) SHOW LIGHTS AFTER DARK.

Answer: ALL of these DORA rules were true.

In 1916, in York, the first person fined was Jim Richardson, who was fined 5 shillings for lighting a cigarette in the street at night. The Zep-panicking magistrate told him that...

A LIGHTED MATCH COULD BE SEEN BY A ZEPPELIN FLYING 2,000 FEET UP

The Rev Patrick Shaw was arrested for showing a light from his church, even though he argued it was only a 'dim religious light'. The Zep-panicking magistrate fined him anyway.

Police also banned loud noises. In York, the Chief Constable told residents…

DO
NOT

- laugh in the streets
- let your dogs bark outside
- bang on doors

All these noises can be heard from a Zeppelin listening for its target.

The man was clearly a Yorkshire pudding. But was he any worse than the newspaper which had the bright idea to light a huge area of empty countryside at night to attract Zeppelins and then destroy them – like moths around a candle flame?

The Zeppelins were called 'baby killers' by the British people. But they were also really easy to hit with guns and aeroplanes – the last raid took place in June 1917.

THE WAR ENDED IN NOVEMBER 1918.

FLYING VISIT TO FIRST WORLD WAR QUIZ

1 The first fighter planes didn't have machine guns. What weapons did the pilots use?

a) Balloons filled with water to soak the enemy cameras

b) Bricks dropped on the heads of the enemy pilots

2 Raymond Collishaw crash-landed at a French farm when he was trying to deliver a love letter to the farmer's daughter. Collishaw lived but the love letter was covered in what?

a) Mashed turnips

b) Cow poo

3 By 1917, the German Air Force had ace pilots, led by Manfred von Richthofen, in a group known as Richthofen's Circus? Why?

a) Because they dressed as clowns and painted their faces
b) Because they painted their planes bright colours

4 Adolphe Pegoud was a French pilot who was shot down by a German pilot, Otto Kandulski, and died. If he'd lived, he'd have been annoyed. Why?

a) Otto was waving a white flag of surrender so Adolphe had spared his life
b) Before the war, Adolphe had taught Otto how to fly

5 Marie Marvingt became a Famous First in 1915. What did she do?

a) Became the first French nurse to be killed by a German bomb
b) Became the first French woman to fly into battle, dressed as a man, and bomb

Answers: all answers are (b).

THE GOLDEN
AGE

As the war created better planes, pilots learned to do amazing tricks and crowds paid to see them risk their lives. In the 1920s and 1930s, they did stunts and broke records for money.

Entertainers walked on wings, fired pistols at targets and even played tennis as they stood on the wings. Many of them also died trying. Some of the forgotten famous were...

FABULOUS FLIERS

Lincoln Beachey (1887–1915)

Lincoln Beachey was just 17 when he first took to the air. He became America's most famous stunt pilot. In one year, 17 million people saw him fly. Beachey...

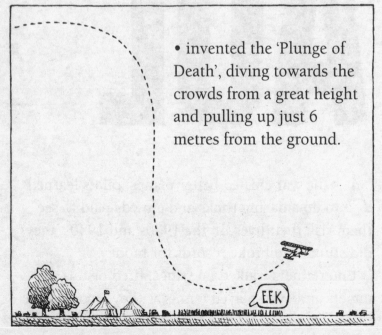

• invented the 'Plunge of Death', diving towards the crowds from a great height and pulling up just 6 metres from the ground.

EEK

• won the $1,000 prize for being the first person to fly over Niagara Falls. (He then flew under the Honeymoon Bridge, just a few metres above the water. Show off.)

• did a loop then went on to break the world record with 80 loops in a row.

• arranged races as the 'demon of the sky' against a sports car driver, the 'daredevil of the ground'. (He sometimes let the car win to make it more fun for the crowds.)

• played out a pretend attack on a huge wooden model of a warship and pretended to blow it up. (The model was packed with explosives and was set off with a fuse but the watching people who screamed and fainted believed Beachey had bombed it.)

• flew over a speeding train and touched the roof of a carriage with his wheels.

★ **PLANE CRAZY?** ★

THEN MAYBE A STUNT PILOT LIFE IS FOR YOU

Send your application by Airmail, of course.

Other young airmen tried to copy his tricks. After 24 of them died and Beachey was so upset he gave up flying for a while. Beachey said the crowds who paid to see him were really cruel.

The crowd got their wish in 1915. Beachey flew over San Francisco Bay, upside down. When the plane started to fly towards the water, he tried to flip it over. He flipped too hard and the wings fell off. He drowned.

BARNSTORMING BRAVES

After the end of the First World War there were a lot of old air force planes going cheap and a lot of young pilots wanting to make their fortunes like Lincoln Beachey.

From early spring until after the harvest and county fairs in the Autumn, these pilots would fly over a small town to grab people's attention. They would then land at a local farm and store their planes in a barn. They became known as 'barnstormers'.

They would pay the farmer to use a field as a runway to give air shows and offer aeroplane rides.

The fliers would zoom over the village and drop leaflets to advertise. They were so popular in the 1920s that a whole town might close down because everyone wanted to watch the stunts.

SEE THE
BARNSTORMING
BRAVES

See spins, dives, loop-the-loops and barrel rolls.

**TAKE
A RIDE
$5 FOR 15
MINUTES**

**Be amazed by feats of wing-walking,
stunt parachuting, mid-air plane crossing from
plane to plane, dancing on the plane's wings.
Watch the braves risk their lives flying into the
doors of the barn and out the other side.**

The truth is they really DID risk their lives when flying through barns. Many crashed and died.

Paul Tibbets (1915–2007)

In 1923, the barnstorming Doug Davis upset a lot of people by flying between tall buildings in Pittsburgh. He dropped sweets on parachutes. A sweet maker paid Davis to take his son up in the plane to drop the sweets. The son was eight-year-old Paul Tibbets.

Paul later said…

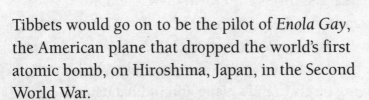

FROM THAT DAY ON, I KNEW I HAD TO FLY

Tibbets would go on to be the pilot of *Enola Gay*, the American plane that dropped the world's first atomic bomb, on Hiroshima, Japan, in the Second World War.

The people on the ground saw a brilliant flash of light – followed by a loud booming sound. Around 70,000–80,000 men, women and children were killed by the blast and firestorm that followed. Another 70,000 were injured. About 5 square miles of the city were destroyed.

Barnstorm to firestorm.

Ormer Locklear (1891–1920)

The more thrills the crowds saw, the more dangerous the pilots had to be. By 1919, the public were saying, 'Wing-walking? Boring. Seen it.' Ormer Locklear swung from a trapeze under the bottom wing of his friend's plane and did handstands on the top wing. Boring. Seen it.

So, Ormer came up with a stunt so daring no one has ever tried in since. The 'Dance of Death'...

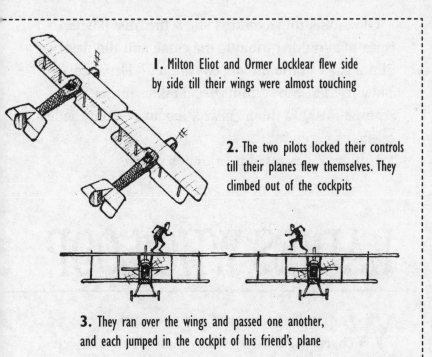

1. Milton Eliot and Ormer Locklear flew side by side till their wings were almost touching

2. The two pilots locked their controls till their planes flew themselves. They climbed out of the cockpits

3. They ran over the wings and passed one another, and each jumped in the cockpit of his friend's plane

Ormer became a movie star, doing stunts for films like *The Great Air Robbery*. But the movies were the death of him. He flew in a plane with Milton Eliot as the pilot. The two friends had to make a steep dive over an oilfield at night. The floodlights lit up the plane, but they had to be switched off at the end of Milton's dive.

The lights stayed on a moment too long and Milton was blinded. He smashed into a pool of oil next to the oil well and they exploded in a fireball.

Of course, they couldn't show the film. They certainly couldn't include the crash and the deaths of the stars in the movie, could they? They did. They used a snip of film they'd taken earlier that seemed to show the men walking away from the crash.

Hollywood wanted its money's worth.

LADIES WHO LOOP

Women had to work hard to join the barnstorming world of men. Some showed how women were as good as men. And some died to prove it.

Harriet Quimby (1875–1912)

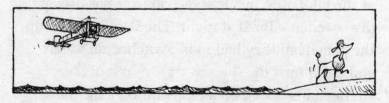

Rose Isabel Spencer was the first woman to fly a powered aircraft – Airship Number 1 at Crystal Palace, London in 1902.

The first woman to earn a pilot license was French woman Raymonde de Laroche in 1910. She died when her plane crashed nine years later.

On the other hand, Harriet Quimby – the first woman in America to earn a pilot license – became a heroine.

• In 1911, Harriet was the first woman in America to get a licence to fly and joined a group of touring air-show pilots.

• She also wrote Hollywood movies and appeared in one.

• On April 16, 1912, Quimby became the first woman to pilot an aircraft across the English Channel. No one noticed because the newspapers were filled with a much bigger story – the *Titanic* sank the day before.

• Three months later she gave an air show in her brand-new plane. At a height of 300 metres, the aircraft suddenly flipped over. Harriet wasn't wearing a seatbelt, she was thrown out of the aircraft and fell to her death. Strangely, the plane glided down and landed itself in a muddy field.

• Harriet died showing the way for women of the time. She said...

There is no reason why the aeroplane should not be a successful job for women. They can make good incomes by carrying passengers between towns, deliver parcels, take photographs from above and teach at schools for flying.

DID YOU KNOW?

Denise Moore became a sad Famous First. She was the first known female flier to die in a plane accident. Her plane turned upside down and she fell 50 metres to the ground.

MY REAL NAME WAS MRS E.J. CORNESSON. I CALLED MYSELF DENISE MOORE TO KEEP MY FAMILY FROM FINDING OUT I WAS FLYING

FASTER AND FURTHER

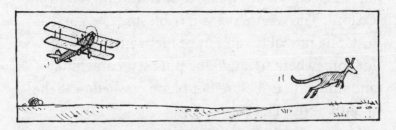

Amy Johnson (1903–1941)

In 1930, Amy Johnson became the first woman to fly solo from England to Australia. She broke many records and was world famous. She is one of the few fliers to have a popular song written about her. It's not a very good song but people enjoyed it...

She's landed in Vienna, Here she is in Baghdad.
Now she's over Karachi, She's reached Port Darwin ... Bravo.
She's up again, she's off to Brisbane, Here she comes, there's something wrong
Gracious, what's wrong? She's crashed, no, she's safe.

Then along came the Second World War and Amy kept flying. She wasn't allowed to fly fighter planes or bombers, but she could fly them to the airfields where the Royal Air Force could take over.

In January 1941, Amy was given the job of flying an Airspeed Oxford plane to RAF Kidlington near Oxford. The weather was terrible and she got lost. She probably ran out of fuel while looking for somewhere to land. She put on a parachute and jumped out before her plane crashed near the mouth of the Thames.

Some warships saw Amy's parachute coming down and saw her alive in the water, calling for help. The seas were rough, and snow was falling. Walter Fletcher, the Captain of HMS *Haslemere*, tried to rescue her. The crew of the ship threw ropes out to Amy, but she couldn't reach them and was lost under the ship. Walter Fletcher dived in and swam out in search of a body in the water. By the time the lifeboat reached him, he was frozen and died in hospital days later.

DID YOU KNOW?

Sixty years after her death, a gunner told a strange tale. He said he was on duty looking for German bombers. He sent a radio signal to a plane that gave the wrong secret password. So he shot it down near the mouth of the Thames. The next day the team of gunners read about Amy's disappearance and they were sure that was who they'd shot down.

THE OFFICERS TOLD US NEVER TO TELL ANYONE WHAT HAPPENED

BANG!

OOPS

Amy's body was never found. The woman who flew around the world and lived through crashes, died just a short distance from a safe British airfield.

Amy, wonderful Amy, I'm proud of the way you flew.
Believe me, Amy, you cannot blame me, Amy,
For falling in love with you.

The record ends with the sound of people cheering.

★ SEE ★

Prisoners in Hull Prison made a copy of Amy's plane
that she flew to Australia. It is in Stephen's Shopping
Centre next to Hull Paragon Station.
The plane that Amy flew is now in the Science
Museum.

Amelia Earhart (1897–1937)

Amelia, an American, was the first woman to fly
solo across the Atlantic Ocean. Her disappearance
was even more mysterious than Amy Johnson's.

In July 1937, she set off to fly around the world. She set off to fly the first part of the flight across the Pacific to an island in the Pacific Ocean. She never arrived.

Some people think she crashed into the sea and others believe she landed on a desert island. Four years later, a US ship found a navigation box on the island. It was the sort Amelia would have used. A British man, Gerald Gallagher, did a search and said he found a skeleton…

Another idea is that she was captured by Japanese soldiers and executed.

The truth is? No one knows and we maybe never will. One song for Amelia comes up with the idea that she's in heaven. That's probably better than being executed…

There's a beautiful, beautiful field,
Far away in a land that is fair
Happy landings to you, Amelia Earhart,
Farewell, first lady of the air.

Bill Lancaster (1898–1933)

Not every disappearing flier stayed a mystery for ever. Bill Lancaster was a hero of the 1930s along with his friend Jessie 'Chubbie' Miller.

In 1927, Chubbie was desperate to become the first woman to fly from the UK to Australia. With the

help of Bill Lancaster, she did it as a passenger. Amy Johnson made that flight as a solo pilot three years later. Amy is remembered, Chubbie is forgotten.

In the 1930s, Chubbie and Bill were famous. They toured the world, then it all went wrong. A

guest at his house in Miami, USA, shot himself. Bill was the last one to see the guest alive and was accused of his murder.

Bill was found not guilty but he was no longer a hero.

What could he do to win back his fans? He decided to break a speed record by flying to South Africa. THAT would get him back the public's favour. In 1933, he took off from the south coast of England with just one reporter and his mum watching. There was no fan club.

His mother handed him a small packet of chicken sandwiches, a bar of chocolate and a flask of coffee for the journey.

Bill was a mummy's boy but no chicken. The plane carried a two-gallon drum of water but no survival supplies.

He became lost and vanished somewhere over the Sahara Desert. Searchers looked for where he might have crash-landed but he was way off course. They couldn't search all 3.5 million square miles of the desert. They gave up and Bill was forgotten.

As for Chubbie? Three years after Bill disappeared...

In 1962, almost 30 years after Bill vanished, a French Army patrol found the wrecked plane and Bill's corpse. It had been dried out in the desert air.

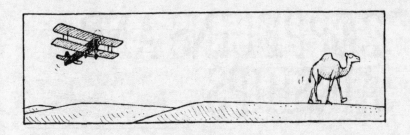

It seems Bill had lived for over a week after the crash. He kept a diary till the end, and it was found beside the plane. The last page said...

So, the beginning of the eighth day has dawned. It is still cool. I have no water... I am waiting patiently. Come soon please. Fever wracked me last night.

Hope you get my full log.

Bill.

The mystery was solved. The soldiers also found a photo beside the body. A photo of Chubbie. They gave Chubbie the diary. Awwww.

ZEPPELINS AND AIRSHIPS

After the First World War, fliers were keen to try airships as peaceful passenger aircraft. In spite of all the lessons about using dangerous (but cheap) hydrogen, the airlines kept on using it.

The R101 Airship
5 October 1930

In the 1920s airships – filled with gas – flew across the Atlantic and over the North Pole. But in 1930, a British airship, R101, came down in France, caught fire and killed 48 people.

The R101 was made from the skins of a million ox guts and was filled with the explosive hydrogen gas. Experts said the safe helium gas would have worked just as well. The government decided that they would use dangerous hydrogen because it was cheaper. Heavy rain over France soaked the R101's gas bag and dragged it down. The airship hit the top of a hill. Six crew were thrown clear and survived. A spark from the engine set the gas alight and no fire service in the world could have put out the hydrogen fire once it started.

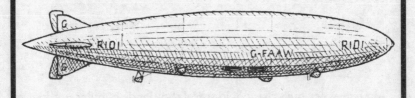

The Hindenburg
6 May 1937

Aircraft are heavier than air and if they lose power the pilot cannot always make a safe landing. But carrying passengers under a floating bag of gas was thought to be much safer.

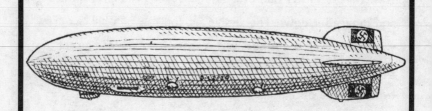

Airships were built that could travel thousands of miles without fear of crashing. The German airship *Hindenburg* was the largest airship ever built at around 250 metres long and, in the year she was built, 1936, covered 186,000 safe miles. On 6 May 1937, she came in to land in New Jersey in the USA after crossing the Atlantic. An electrical spark probably started the fire that caught the inflammable hydrogen in the gas bag and she sank to the ground in a ball of fire.

Amazingly, only 35 of the 97 people aboard died. An American radio commentator was making a live broadcast of the landing and his horrified report has never been forgotten. 'This is the worst thing I've ever witnessed,' he sobbed.

Why did the airship explode? Because it didn't use safe helium gas. Some people never learn from horrible history.

After these disasters people believed airships were dangerous.
And that's why we fly in aeroplanes.

SECOND WORLD WAR

FASTER, HIGHER, STRONGER

In 1896, a Frenchman organized the first modern Olympic games and said the motto was 'Citius, Altius, Fortius'. He was just showing off, using Latin. What it meant was 'faster, higher, stronger'. And faster, higher, stronger was the way aircraft were going.

- In 1918, Britain's fastest plane in the First World War was the Sopwith Dragon, which had a top speed of 150 mph.

- In 1945, Britain's fastest plane was the Spitfire that reached 606 mph – FOUR times as fast. (Germany had a rocket-driven fighter that would do 700 mph but only for about 25 miles, so it wasn't much use.)

As for the terror of bombers…

- In 1918, the Handley Page O/100 Bomber could carry 2,000 pounds of bombs.

- In 1945, the Avro Lancaster carried over 20,000 pounds of bombs – more than TEN times as much.

HIGH SPY

General Han Xin had wanted to see what the enemy was doing on the far side of the hill and used kites. In the Second World War, British spies could do better. They could fly over enemy land, drop by parachute at night and live there.

They could report on the enemy by radio. That's the best way to spy.

The German army had taken over France. Some of the French formed a freedom-fighter army – the Resistance – to attack the German army inside France.

This was possible because of aeroplanes. Spies could be sent with the supplies. But no one could know who these spies were ... not even in Britain. This secret army had to stay secret.

The British set up the secret 'Operation Carpetbagger'. (A 'carpetbagger' was someone who carried all they needed in a small bag – they were not there to stay.)

Not everyone was pleased to see the new Carpetbaggers. They took over the British Air Force airfield at Harrington, so the usual pilots had to move out. When they left, they dropped hundreds of toilet rolls over the camp.

Spies who were being sent to France arrived at Harrington in large American cars with curtains across the windows. They were hidden in huts and dressed in padded suits.

No one was allowed to see or talk to them. Just before take-off the spies were taken to the plane.

Special planes called Lysanders were used. While the warplanes were getting faster, the Lysanders were extra slow, so they could land on small fields and take off quickly. That was useful, but if they met an enemy fighter plane they would have little chance of escape.

It was dangerous work for the spies and the pilots, landing in French fields where German patrols might spot them. The Carpetbaggers had a lot of success. 556 agents were landed, and 4,500 tons of supplies dropped. But many planes were lost and 208 aircrew members were killed or captured in over 3,000 flights.

★ SEE ★

Carpetbagger Aviation Museum, Harrington, Northamptonshire. Open weekends.

FIRESTORM FURY

In the Second World War, the German leader ordered that his air force bomb London and other British cities. The British hit back and bombed cities in Germany.

War is horrible but the Second World War was especially horrible because so many millions of innocent civilians were killed, some bombed in their homes, miles away from battle front. Aeroplanes made that possible.

London was bombed for 57 nights in a row from 7 September 1940. In Britain over 40,000 people died in The Blitz.

Here are just ten gruesome facts about a bombing raid when the enemy destroyed a city without mercy.

February 1945

1 It was Shrove Tuesday and a carnival day. A day for children to forget the ongoing war, dress up in bright costumes and have a parade through the city streets. The circus was performing to a thousand happy families and there was no warning of what was to come.

2 First came the 'pathfinder' planes. They found the city and dropped red marker bombs that hovered 200 metres above the city centre and marked the way for the explosive bombers. Home Defence Fighters took off to shoot them down but the panicking gunners on the ground shot down their own planes. People who saw the flares ran for cover and the shelter of the cellars. But no air raid siren sounded.

3 The last act of the circus began and clowns rode donkeys into the ring. That's when the warnings finally rang out.

THE FIRST WAVES OF A LARGE ENEMY BOMBER FORMATION HAVE CHANGED COURSE AND ARE NOW APPROACHING THE CITY BOUNDARIES. THERE IS GOING TO BE AN ATTACK. YOU ARE INSTRUCTED TO GO AT ONCE TO THE BASEMENTS AND CELLARS. THE POLICE HAVE INSTRUCTIONS TO ARREST ALL THOSE WHO REMAIN IN THE OPEN

4 At 10:13 p.m. the first bombs fell. They were shattering high explosives that brought down buildings and trapped citizens in their shelters below the ground. But the worst was still to come. The fires sucked in air, greedy for oxygen, and winds rushed to feed them. The fires grew hotter, sucked harder, and the winds grew stronger and stronger and stronger. This was the firestorm effect the bombers wanted. It was a whirlwind of flames that uprooted trees and sucked people off their feet into the heart of a fire.

5 The next wave of bombers arrived at 1:30 a.m. in the morning and they were carrying fire-bombs that spread a blazing liquid over the city and turned it into a massive bonfire. They had no trouble finding the city. They could see the fires caused by the first wave from 200 miles away. This time the home fighter planes stayed on the ground. No one knows why – some think the links to their aerodrome were cut. The bombers had the freedom of the skies to drop their deadly fire-bombs wherever they wanted. Of the 1,400 enemy aircraft that flew over the city that night only six failed to return. As the circus tent collapsed in flames, the dappled grey Arab horses huddled in a frightened circle. Their glittering costumes were seen shimmering in the light of the fires.

6 The next day dawned. Ash Wednesday – some citizens must have smiled grimly at that name as survivors crawled out of the rubble that was once a city centre. A three-mile cloud of yellow-brown smoke drifted over the city and carried charred debris that fell on a prisoner of war camp 15 miles away. Then the third flight of bombers arrived to rain down a further 11 minutes of death. Long range enemy fighters flew low and machine-gunned anything or anyone that moved. One plane machine-gunned a children's choir.

7 The people in the cellars had weakened the walls that joined their house to the ones next door. When their escape to the street was blocked, they broke down the walls into other houses again and again, looking for a way out. But smoke from the fires rolled down and choked them. An army officer, home on leave, saw 60 people in a cellar, their escape barred by a fire. He tried to help them…

The ones who refused to take his advice died.

8 One of the main targets had been the train station. That morning children's bodies were stacked there in a huge mound. Many were still wearing their bright carnival costumes. But the station wasn't destroyed. By the next day the trains were running again. So tens of thousands of people had died and the enemy had gained very little.

9 Then the job of counting the cost began. For a week after the raid the city was filled with unburied dead. Bodies were lined up on the pavement to be identified. Rescue workers were given cigarettes and brandy to mask the smell. Prisoners of war were brought in to help with the work – but the citizens attacked them. They had to take their revenge out on someone.

10 Bodies were buried in mass graves but there were no coffins and no sheets. Many were simply wrapped in newspapers, some in empty paper cement bags. There were too many dead to count. Some guesses say that it was 135,000 in just a couple of days of fire and terror but the true number was probably 25,000. Still a terrible suffering.

This wasn't London destroyed by Nazi monsters. This was Dresden in Germany, bombed by the British RAF by night and the US Air Force by day.

Britain lost around 40,000 people to German bombing. Germany lost around 600,000. So, who won the war of the bombers?

EPILOGUE

Human beings are the cleverest animals on the planet. The trouble is that one person may invent something wonderful that will make life better for everyone. Then another person comes along and says...

AHA. I CAN USE THAT INVENTION TO BE CRUEL OR WICKED OR TO MAKE MYSELF RICH

Invent ships? You have pirates. Invent trains? You have train robbers. Invent cars? You have ram-raiders. Invent planes? You have a load of new crimes. Crimes like taking over the plane in mid-air: hijacking.

Aircraft can be used to take you anywhere you want to go, to rescue people and put out fires, to take supplies to hungry people and to learn more about our planet. Good old aircraft.

They can also be used – as Orville Wright said – to kill people in their thousands with bullets and bombs. Bad old aircraft.

It wasn't long before they were being used to break the law. Soon after the first planes were flying, they were being used to smuggle whisky from the USA into Mexico. All the border fences and guards in the world couldn't stop them.

Look at some of the flight crimes there have been in just over a hundred years of powered flight.

JAIL BIRDS

There have been hundreds of hijackings.

• In 1932, three rebels took a hostage and made him climb aboard a transport plane. None of the men had flown a plane before, yet they managed to take off...

They crashed and all four men died.

• The word 'hijack' may have come from highway robbers in the USA who would stop a lorry and say...

• In 1976, a really stupid hijacker jumped from his seat, pointed a gun at the stewardess and said...

• Some hijacks have worked. In the 1960s, a gunman held an airliner and its passengers to ransom on the runway. He asked for $200,000 and four parachutes. He got both, then ordered the pilot to take off. By the time the plane landed the man was gone. He took the parachute to freedom somewhere over mid-west America and was never caught.

• In 1985, an ex-convict hijacked a Norwegian Boeing 737 armed with a pistol. He decided to give up his plan so long as the police were willing to give him one thing: beer. In the end, the plane landed safely at the airport in Oslo, none of the 115 passengers on board were harmed, and the hijacker was arrested.

Planes?

A good thing or a bad thing?

DEPENDS WHAT YOU USE THEM FOR

INTERESTING INDEX

Abbas ibn Firnas (Spanish inventor) 17-19, 50-1

aeroplanes 38, 40, 52-3, 59, 66, 80-1, 84-5, 94, 121, 127

air crashes 7, 21, 25-6, 30
  and barnstormers 103, 106-11
  and hijackings 136
  a lot of 32, 34, 40-2, 48, 52, 58, 62, 64, 67, 70-1, 75-6, 79, 113, 116-17, 120
  quiz questions about 95

air raids, atrocious 87, 89, 94, 127-8, 132

airships (bags of gas) 33-4, 57, 59, 87-8, 106, 118-21

Alcock, John (British flier) 66-7, 66-8, 66-9, 66-71

animals, aloft 15, 21, 23, 47-8

balloons 9, 80, 88
  barrage 35-6

loony 22-36, 47-8

Barber, Horatio (British inventor) 40-1

barking, banned 93

barnstormers, bizarre 101-4

Beachey, Lincoln (American stunt pilot) 98-101

bed, falling out of 7

Blanchard, Jean-Pierre (French balloonist) 26-9, 31, 47-8

Blanchard, Sophie (French balloonist) 31-2

Bleriot, Louis (French flier) 60-6

Blitz, The 35, 77, 127

Bocker, Alois (German captain) 87

bombers, bonkers 35, 67, 110-11, 123, 127-30, 128, 133

bombs 35, 126
  atomic 77, 103-104
  breaking law 135
  in First World War 67, 87, 89, 96, 99, 123

in Second World War 35, 126-33, 127, 129-30
  as souvenirs 91
boys, brave 37-9, 76, 103
Brown, Arthur (British flier) 66-7, 66-8, 66-9, 66-71
bullets 85-6, 135

Carpetbaggers, cranky 124-6
Cayley, George (British inventor) 37-8, 40
children 45, 72, 91, 104, 127, 130-1
Cocking, Robert (British parachutist) 49-50
crime 72-3, 134-5

daredevils 9, 52, 99
De Lagarde, Miss (French balloonist) 30
De Rozier, Jean-François Pilâtre (French balloonist) 23-6, 30
Death 26, 32, 72, 105-7, 111
  Dance of 104-5
  in firestorms 130, 132
  Plunge of 98
dirigibles (flying machines) 57-9
DORA (Defence of the Realm Act) 89-92

Earhart, Amelia (American flier) 112-14
Eiffel Tower (French monument) 34, 53, 57-8
Eilmer, Brother (English inventor) 19-20
Eliot, Milton (American stunt pilot) 105
epilogue (ending) 134-8

Famous Firsts 8-9, 16, 26, 29
  aeroplanes 38
  air raids 87
  balloonists 33, 39
  barnstormers 99, 104
  fines 92
  glider flights 40
  modern Olympics 122
  non-stop flights 66-9
  over water 47, 60-3

parachute jumps 49-51
plane controls 65
powered flights 74, 76-80
quiz questions 95-6
solo flights 27, 71, 109, 112, 115
timing gear 96
women fliers 30-2, 106-9, 112-14
fighter planes, frightening 1, 85-7, 95, 110, 123, 126, 128-30
firestorms, fried in 126-33
fireworks 12
First World War, flying further in 67, 71, 77, 84-96, 100, 123
French Resistance (freedom fighters) 124
French Revolution, furious 23

Giffard, Henri (French balloonist) 33-4
gliders glorious 37-43, 75
Golden Age, of flying 97-121

Hamilton, Charles (American flier) 52-3
Han Xin (Chinese general) 12-13, 85
Health Warning, helpful 25
helicopters 79, 81
hijackings, hellish 134, 136-7
Hindenburg (German airship) 119-21

Icarus (Greek jumper) 15
Icarus II (pig that flew) 15

Jeffries, John (American balloonist) 26-9
Johnson, Amy (British flier) 109-12, 115
jumpers, with wings 9, 15-21

kites, crazy 10-14, 76, 90, 123

Labrosse, Jeanne G. (French balloonist) 31
Lancaster, Bill (British flier) 114-17
Latham, Hubert (French flier) 62-4
laughing, banned 93

Law, Frederick R. (American parachutist) 49
Lilenthal, Otto (German glider pilot) 41–2
Lindbergh, Charles (American flier) 71–3
Locklear Ormer (American stunt pilot) 104–5
loops, looping the 99, 102, 106

Miller, Jessie 'Chubbie' (Australian flier) 114–17
models, making 53–5, 75–6
Montalembert, Countess of (French balloonist) 30
Montgolfier Brothers (French balloon makers) 23–4
museums, musty 43, 65, 70, 78, 112, 126

ornithopters (flapping flying machines) 61

parachutes, precious 9, 31, 44–55, 81, 110, 123, 137
Pearse, Richard (New Zealand inventor) 78–80
Pilcher, Percy (British glider pilot) 42–3
Podenas, Countess of (French balloonist) 30
poetry, putrid 18
police 93, 128, 137
powered flight 33, 40, 43, 74–83, 82–3, 135
prizes 56–73
propellers 33, 44, 64, 79, 85

Quimby, Harriet (American flier) 106–8
quiz, quick 95–6

railways 8, 33
Reichelt, Franz (Austrian inventor) 48–9
Romain, Pierre (French balloonist) 24

safety 7–10
Santos-Dumont, Alberto (Brazilian pilot) 57–60
Second World War, scary 35, 77, 104, 110, 122–33
smuggling 135
songs, sickening 30, 45–6, 109, 111, 113–14
sound, speed of 77
spies, secretive 123–6

teachers, trying 25, 51, 53
Thible, Élisabeth (French balloonist) 30
Tibbets, Paul (American stunt pilot) 103–4
timing gears, invented 85–6
Titanic (sinking ship) 8, 107

Warren, Edward (American balloonist) 39
Whitehead, Gustave (German flier) 80–2
wind tunnels, turbulent 75
wings 51, 61, 81
    falling off 100
    handstands on 104
    jumping with 9
    melting 15
    running on 105
    wacky 16–17, 19, 37, 40, 42
    walking on 72, 97–8, 102, 104
women, wonderful 9, 30–3, 72, 96, 104, 106–17
Woodrow, Bertie (British chauffeur) 40–1
Wright Brothers (American fliers) 65–6, 74–8

Zeppelin, Ferdinand (German inventor) 87
Zeppelins (airships) 87–9, 91–4, 92–3, 118

TERRY DEARY

Terry Deary was born at a very early age, so long ago he can't remember. But his mother, who was there at the time, says he was born in Sunderland, north-east England, in 1946 – so it's not true that he writes all *Horrible Histories* from memory. At school he was a horrible child only interested in playing football and giving teachers a hard time. His history lessons were so boring and so badly taught, that he learned to loathe the subject. *Horrible Histories* is his revenge.

MARTIN BROWN

M artin Brown was born in Melbourne, on the proper side of the world. Ever since he can remember he's been drawing. His dad used to bring back huge sheets of paper from work and Martin would fill them with doodles and little figures. Then, quite suddenly, with food and water, he grew up, moved to the UK and found work doing what he's always wanted to do: drawing doodles and little figures.

LOOK OUT FOR

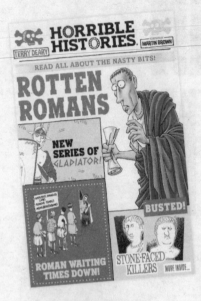